un
stuck

FOR WOMEN

Break Free From Self-Doubt and **Stop Overthinking** Using **The Spiral Stopper Method** To Take Control of Your Emotions, Build **Confidence & Self Love**

BY CHRISTY HOLT

ISBN: 978-1-7386439-4-3

www.gtfu.ca

Table of Contents

Who this Book is For

This book is for the whole-ass human who is ready to get the fuck unstuck and become a powerful conscious creator, designing their own life experiences.

As a whole-ass human, you may currently be experiencing any or all of the following types of challenges that are currently keeping you from experiencing more of what it is you truly desire.

Perhaps you regularly deal with anxious thoughts and emotions:

- Overthinking everything you say or do
- Stressing the fuck out over everything big or small

- Feeling overwhelmed by uncertainty and paralyzed by your fears
- Trash talking yourself and being hypercritical
- Pondering your ability to be both *too much* and *not enough* at the same time
- Experiencing a repetitive loop of thoughts and emotions
- Attempting to control your environment, circumstances or other people

It may feel like you're stuck living on autopilot:

- Sick and tired of seeing the patterns repeating, yet finding yourself perpetuating them
- Uncomfortable existing within your current circumstances yet unsure how to change them

- Unable to get the changes you desire to stick, despite your very best intentions
- Thinking that although things "could be worse", they could also be so much better

You want to move forward, but you're:

- Unsure why you don't have the motivation that others seem to
- Hung up on wanting to know all of the *how* before you start to move forward
- Exhausted or burnt out from actively trying to do ALL OF THE THINGS yet getting nowhere fast

As a result you may also be experiencing interpersonal challenges such as:

- Dealing with regular unnecessary or unresolved conflict in relationship
- Putting the needs of others ahead of your own and then feeling underappreciated
- Hesitating to ask others for what you want and need, not wanting to be a burden
- Being triggered or offended easily by the words or behaviors of others
- Having difficulty managing expectations of others, often feeling let down
- Putting up walls to protect yourself from getting hurt
- Repeating patterns of trying to be good enough such as perfectionism and people-pleasing

- Wearing masks because you're afraid that if others knew the "real you" they wouldn't like you

Ultimately, you want nothing more than to feel safe and supported. Your soul seeks to be fully seen, heard, loved and accepted. The reason you're NOT able to have this more ideal experience is not because there is something wrong with you or because you have done something wrong. Quite the contrary.

What has often happened here is that you have experienced a survival mode (fight, flight or freeze) response. This is an automatic physiological reaction which activates the nervous system and when experienced in small doses, is completely healthy, helpful and normal. However, when this reaction persists for too long without having an opportunity to return to calmer physiological states, it can have negative effects on both the body and the brain. This is often why you will become triggered and feel out of control, but it's not YOU - it's your physiology!

Thankfully neuroscience shows us that we continue to have neuroplasticity (an ability to change our brain) throughout our entire lives, so it's never too late to change what's not been working!

By implementing the spiral stopping tools in this book you CAN biohack your physiology, gain control over your overwhelming thoughts and create significant change, both inside and out.

You can:

Change yourself

- Break free from unnecessary suffering
- Feel more in control of the life you're creating
- Understand yourself better in order to intentionally create your highest identity
- Look and feel better in your body
- Deepen your spiritual journey

Change your experience

- Update your subconscious programming to support your desired experiences, become more confident and unfuckwithable

- Change your perception of reality, experiencing greater possibilities and opportunities
- Become a conscious creator in your life, intentionally creating all of the happiness, peace, success and abundance that you desire
- Improve your relationships with yourself and others

Change the world

- Give back generously to others
- Create a legacy
- Leave the world a better place

You can create everything you desire in this life and more. Your time is now!

Why this Book

You may or may not know me as I am now - a Happiness Coach living her best life - but in the past I too have been captive to a never-ending spiral of thoughts.

Quite honestly, we don't know what we don't know. You may not yet realize the full magnitude of your stuckness, but there is likely something deep within you that is nudging you to take a step towards creating a better experience for yourself. You should be so proud of yourself for trusting your intuition and following this nudge! This just may be one of the best decisions you've made!

Not so long ago, I was stuck. On the outside, it looked like I had it all: a husband, three kids, my dream house, a business built on passion, and a tonne of friends...but on the inside I was a mess. I was overwhelmed, anxious, stressed out, unhappy, and experiencing several unexplained health symptoms. At times, my thoughts would truly spiral and leave me feeling utterly hopeless about what was to come.

My outlook on life has generally been very positive (in fact, I have been accused of wearing rose-coloured glasses on more than one occasion), but I have also experienced some pretty dark times in my inner world.

Several years ago I felt very disconnected from my then-husband, which left me feeling unwanted and alone despite having plenty of "friends". I felt as though I didn't have anyone who truly saw or understood me.

As a former people-pleaser and perfectionist who believed that her worth came from doing and giving to others, my self-worth was at a critical low. It seemed that no matter how much I gave, I never seemed to be enough. I felt completely trapped in my life and I lacked the confidence to make a change. I was terrified that I would make the wrong decision and so I stayed, paralyzed by indecision for years.

Leaving my marriage of over a decade wasn't a decision I took lightly, and my biggest concern was the impact on my kids.

For a long time I had been waiting for something to change: for the kids to grow up, for my partner to change, some sort of clear direction...I was waiting for a miracle! While I know that miracles can and do happen every single day, what I *didn't* realize then was that by sitting around waiting for something outside of me to change, I had relinquished my personal power.

By waiting for change to happen outside of myself, I was essentially giving up all of the real ability that I did have to make a change happen in my life. I didn't see it that way at the time, but we all know that hindsight is 20/20.

The hard truth is that the experience I was living wasn't anyone else's fault but my own.

While I was busy focusing on my experiences of frustration, sadness, loneliness and bitterness, I missed some critical life-changing facts. In this book I'll be sharing many of the crucial perception shifts that can affect massive transformation in anyone's life.

Sometimes in life, we change because *we want to*, and other times we change because **we have to**. Changing because we want to is usually far better for us, but since we are human we often choose the "easier" way over the better way. I'll talk about why making lasting change can be so difficult soon, but for now, back to my story.

The reality of it is that it took me getting sick and fucking tired of my own bullshit before I decided to finally make the changes that I needed to make. I was exhausted because I was using SO much energy in order to "hold it all together" on the outside, and it left very little energy to fight the battles of my mind. The score of this matchup was something like:

My Mind - Eleventy Gazillion, Me - 0.

I suffered from poor quality sleep, woke up already overwhelmed by my thoughts, and made it through my day but for the grace of God and strong coffee. I was barely functional. My exhaustion contributed to the divide growing in my marriage at the time and often what was probably a small thing got blown out of proportion into a seemingly giant mountain, impossible to overcome. My busy mind filled in any empty space with stories and assumptions. Unconscious living (aka autopilot mode) ruled the show for me.

When my mind wasn't anxiously running through my endless to-do list, my thoughts were often consumed with "worst-case scenario" this and "you suck" that. As so many people do, I generally see the best in others yet I would often compare others' best sides to the worst sides of myself. Comparison can be a trap that creates unnecessary emotional suffering. By the way, you are meant to be YOU, not anyone else!

I had learned through a lifetime of experiences that others often did not have the capacity or willingness to hold space for my big feelings and thus responded in ways that left me feeling even more alone. Rather than realizing this had to do with *their emotional intelligence (or lack thereof)* and nothing to do with me or my feelings being unacceptable, I chalked it up to another one of my shortcomings: I was *too much.*

Everything felt incongruent because I was simultaneously *not enough* and *too much*. It was an impossible goal of perfection that kept me stuck in the loop of people-pleasing and doing all of the things, yet *never fucking getting anywhere.* How the fuck could I ever fix this?!

As I look back now, I can see that I was living unconsciously, rather unaware of what was truly happening while my mind ran on autopilot. It is a common tendency to allow our past experiences, thoughts, and emotions to create both our experience and our identity. A big part of the world is "functioning" this way, yet this is certainly not an ideal mode of operation.

Operating in mere survival mode, my energy was often drained by things that did not make me feel good and I had experience after experience that I did not wish to have. I had allowed and tolerated, and even *invited* into my experience, far too many experiences that I did NOT want to be having.

Not only did I have low energy, but I felt lost and without purpose. My self-worth had taken a nosedive after years of absorbing the negative words of others and allowing my thoughts and emotions to run wild continued to fuel that experience. I had inexplicable emotional responses and was often confused and ashamed of my thoughts and responses.

To this point, I had let my past experiences create the same version of reality on repeat. At least I was consistent: each experience based upon these past expectations and assumptions would measure up to the vision I had first created with my thoughts. As expected, fear of future uncertainties ruled my days and kept me stuck in a perpetual loop of suffering.

If I'm honest with you, I can say that I lived in a fog of unconscious experience for far too long. It seemed far too difficult to face the uncertainty of change. I had to reach a breaking point before I could snap myself out of it.

I had believed for a long time that keeping our family together was the best choice for the children. I was desperate to put their needs first, despite the obvious toll on me. I would have done whatever it took for them to be okay, but I was continually playing the role of martyr. In retrospect, this was simply an excuse to avoid making the changes that I truly needed to make. In the end, what shifted was that while I knew I needed to make changes for myself, it was even more important that I made those changes for them.

Awareness is a beautiful thing. Once I became aware of what was happening, I realized that I was done putting up with it. With this new awareness, I knew that I needed to set a better example for my children.

I needed to show my children how to truly love themselves and others and that they alone are responsible for creating their happiness. The only way to accomplish this goal was by leading by example. What I needed first was to get the fuck unstuck.

So, the journey began. Little by little, I slowly built more confidence as I learned to not only accept but to trust my unique skills and gifts. I started to explore who I am and what I truly desire. It certainly has been an enlightening journey of personal discovery, one that has yet to end.

Over the years I have worked with a number of coaches and psychologists, read countless books, and absorbed teachings from a plethora of sources. I have done the research the long and slow way, and I am passionate about sharing what I've learned so that you can get the fuck unstuck much more quickly and easily. Basically, I want to share the cheat codes and hacks so that you don't have to spend years figuring it all out like I did.

As for myself, I continue to peel back the layers. It is an adventure of daily discovery, learning more and more about who I am. I am continuously taking a closer look at the conditioning and masks that I had unconsciously built my identity upon which no longer serve my highest good. I now prioritize taking exceptional care of my mind, body and soul, loving and accepting myself and others, setting and maintaining clear boundaries, and manifesting my dreams.

At times the changes have been subtle, but other times I have experienced such giant shifts that have left me in awe. I have built a business that I adore, created a daily experience of fun and adventure and I even found the most amazing partner in crime. He's my bestest friend and my biggest cheerleader...and as a bonus, all these years later we still can't keep our hands off each other. My life is far from perfect, but I think it's pretty darn perfect for me, and that's what counts.

Looking back from this new higher viewpoint, I can confidently say that I'm a completely different person now, barely recognizable from the lonely and anxious mom I was all those years ago. I can't wait to share some of the most crucial bits of knowledge that have the power to change YOUR life, too.

When I was stuck, my thoughts ran out of control. I felt anxious and overwhelmed by them ALL THE TIME. By learning how to stop the spiral, I have enabled myself to intentionally create the experience of balance and peace. You can create this experience for yourself, too.

When I was stuck, I felt helpless to influence my circumstances and thought that things would never change. By making some simple perspective shifts, I have expanded my capacity to powerfully and intentionally create my experiences according to my desires. You can become a conscious creator, too.

When I was stuck, the world seemed to be conspiring against me. But with a mind that is less cluttered with overwhelming debris, I can see more clearly the lessons and growth that remind me that everything is *always* working towards the highest good. You can transform your current mess into your highest best, too.

When I was stuck, I felt like I was somehow simultaneously too much and not good enough. Since I shut down all that negative self-talk swarming around my brain, I now have a deep comfort in knowing that I am perfectly imperfect just as I am, flaws and all. You are perfectly imperfect just as you are, too.

When I was stuck, I would struggle with uncertainty because it made me feel fearful, like I was out of control. Since stopping the spirals, I have learned to not only be at peace with uncertainty, but also to embrace it. What is certain is limited, but we are meant to be limitless. You can embrace the limitless possibilities that exist in the uncertain, too.

It's time to take back your power and start creating more of the experiences that your soul longs to have, and it all starts with the spiral stopper. Are you ready to get the fuck unstuck and become a conscious creator?

I sure hope that your answer to that question was a resounding YES!

Say it aloud with me:

'I'm ready to get the fuck unstuck and to become a conscious creator!'

Perspective is Everything

Before we dig in further I wanted to explain a few important concepts that have the potential to shift your perspectives (and thus your experiences) quickly.

You're not broken. You're human. Stop apologizing.

Contrary to popular belief, healing isn't about fixing yourself. The truth is you're not broken, you're a complex human who has an unlimited capacity for experience. Healing is about loving and accepting all parts of yourself just as you are, even if *(especially when!)* you're not yet where you'd like to be. It's time to stop apologizing for being magnificently human and start embracing yourself, flaws and all!

Duality

We live in a world built upon duality - up and down, big and small, good and bad. For something to exist, there must also be 'nothing'. To define our experience of something, we must have the language to describe it and a reference point or some criteria to be met. For example, in order for us to have a reference point for "big", we must also understand what "small" is. The truth is, none of these descriptors are absolute - they all exist on a spectrum.

Even more importantly, all experience simply IS until we label it and attach meaning to it. There are no universal truths, all that exists simply 'is' until it is perceived and judged. It is your perception which creates your personalized version of "reality", and how you experience that which simply 'is'.

In the highest sense, all experiences are rooted in either love or fear. Fear acts to keep you "safe" inside your comfort zone of familiar experiences - it feels restrictive and small. Love, on the other hand, is expansive and limitless. You are not here to suffer. In fact, quite the opposite!

The best part is that you already have the tools you need to break free from all unnecessary suffering - they already exist within YOU.

You are Creating your Reality with Your Thoughts

Nothing happens in your perceived reality that did not first originate as a thought. Your thoughts are incredibly powerful, and if you are not conscious (aware) of your thoughts, you may be creating that which you do NOT want, rather than what you do want. It is this powerful skill of creation that we must harness in order to intentionally create more of the experiences we desire.

What you believe to be true will be made true by your actions, whether it be conscious or subconscious. So, it's important to get curious about how we might shift our thoughts to create an experience more congruent with what we truly desire.

YOU are the Observer

You are not your thoughts, you are merely the observer of them. You can observe your thoughts as they come and go and as a conscious creator, you have the power to choose which ones you allow to create your experience. Without your judgements, your thoughts carry no weight and they can easily float away as quickly as they came into your mind, creating space for you to select those higher thoughts that support your desired experience instead.

You are not your emotions, you are merely the observer of them. When you physically experience your emotions (energy in motion) in your body as a conscious creator, you have the power to choose which thoughts and stories you attach to them. Without your stories and meanings, your emotions simply exist as information and typically pass very quickly. As a conscious creator, you can objectively examine your emotions and allow them to flow through you, allowing you to feel them *without getting trapped in the spiral.*

You are not your body, you are energy and that energy cannot be contained in just your flesh and bones. Your body is made up of energy, vibrating fast enough that it *appears* to be solid. The reality is that you are *mostly made up of empty space between energy particles.* You are so much greater than the meat suit you're currently embodying, and as a conscious creator, you have the power to choose how you will experience your life while in this human body. You can learn to love and appreciate your body, and use the strengths and gifts it provides for creating the highest and best experience for yourself. Even your perceived flaws are spectacularly designed just for you and can often contain gifts and lessons for you and your highest self.

Who you *Really* are

You are a human being, not a human doing. Your superpower is in being YOU, not in what you DO. There is nothing that you need to DO, rather your purpose is simply to create the experiences that you desire.

Ultimately, there is no right or wrong experience, just what is correct for you.

You are inherently worthy simply for being YOU, and there is always more happiness, more peace, more fun, more love, and more success to experience.

The only thing stopping you from experiencing more is YOU.

Isn't it about time you stopped cockblocking yourself?

Your Mind is an Asshole

There is a reason that you struggle to make lasting change, and it's not because your ex or your boss is an asshole, it's because your *mind* can be an asshole.

Your brain is a high-powered machine filtering through something like a gazillion potential data points per second and choosing which if any data points are relevant and necessary to your immediate current experience. There are an infinite amount of possibilities that exist, but your brain simply cannot handle all of the data and so it does you a solid and filters out that which it deems is irrelevant. Yay! Our brains don't explode from being overloaded.

But, stay with me because this is where it gets interesting.

Your mind is simply doing its job: keeping you safe and filtering into your experience WHATEVER IS A MATCH FOR YOUR DESIRES. You've trained your fancy pants filter (this filter is called the reticular activating system, the RAS) to *seek out that which aligns with what you believe is true.* Basically what gets filtered in is what matches your expectations and assumptions, much like an automatic confirmation bias.

"So you're telling me that my RAS is filtering in what it believes I want to see and experience, but that can't be true!! I don't *want* to keep experiencing suffering and pain!" you might say.

It's uncomfortable as fuck to think that you're somehow driving this bus to a suffer-fest of your own making. I know, because I've been there and driven around on that ratchety old bus, too. Now it's time to change all of that - let's get off the bus and unpack this, shall we?

Without intentional new input, your RAS will continue to filter out what is deemed unnecessary and create a personalized lens of perception for the creation of your reality. *This will run on autopilot with no additional input necessary. When running on autopilot mode, this filter is operating based on your past thoughts, experiences, emotions and memories. Basically, it's serving to recreate your past over and over.*

It's no wonder you find yourself stuck in a perpetual groundhog day. You ARE stuck in a perpetual experience of, well, the same old shit. And the longer you live your life on autopilot, the more your mind thinks "Yes! More of this!" and as you experience, think and feel the same things, these less than desirable neural pathways in your brain become more deeply ingrained, creating bigger and bigger ruts that can eventually seem impossible to get out of.

This may sound kinda defeatist but not to worry! Remember, you are NOT your mind! You are a powerful observer and a conscious creator with the power to rewire your brain (how fucking cool is THAT?!). Huzzah!

It's just that your mind is quite like a self-driving car, and if you don't take the time to set a new destination, you can easily get stuck looping around that one familiar block in your neighborhood. It's time that you set a new destination for yourself - Happiness! Bliss! Peace! Success! Abundance! - and get on your way!

Your Willingness

Before we dive into the strategies for stopping the spiral and overcoming your overwhelming thoughts, it is important to check-in and ask one extremely important question:

Are you willing and ready to experience more?

If your answer is a resounding "fuck yes", then read on my friend, because it's time to create YOUR spiral stopper!

Stop the Spiral!

To get yourself off of autopilot, let's take a brief look at how and why you may be operating in this way. Often as a result of experiencing trauma and/or chronic stress, we can end up operating in survival mode. It's like an all-hands-on-deck sort of situation for dealing with trauma and stress, but our ability to function well is impeded because all of our energy is sucked into the vortex of simply trying to stay alive. The longer you have functioned in survival mode, the more your thoughts and reality have adjusted to this experience. It is a self-fulfilling prophecy that you alone have the ability to break yourself free of!

In your attempt to merely survive, you may have been duped into thinking that having more power or control is the answer. However, in order to make any significant lasting changes, what we first need is for our entire nervous system to stop throwing itself into a toddler-sized tantrum of fight or flight. We must first create safety within our bodies in order to be able to really start making lasting change.

The key purpose of the spiral stopper is to interrupt the patterns that have been keeping you stuck so that you can finally see things with a fresh and more supportive lens. But first and foremost, it's a set of tools that will help you to create (*for yourself)* the safety required in order to have new experiences.

When to Use your Spiral Stopper

We all have those repetitive thoughts that start us off and quickly send us into a spiral. You know, *the ones*. At first, it is simply a passing thought or idea, maybe even an emotion you're feeling in your body. But before you know it, you're in full-fledged meltdown mode questioning why nobody likes you and how your life got so out of control.

You are going to use your spiral stopper *whenever these initial thoughts or feelings pop up* to:

- Regulate your nervous system and create personal safety
- Stop the spiral before it starts

- Allow those overwhelming thoughts and emotions to move THROUGH you while avoiding being consumed by the spiral

By stopping the spiral, you effectively avoid creating further thoughts and emotions that solidify and amplify experiences that do not serve you or your highest good. In releasing attachment to our thoughts and emotions, we can observe them more objectively without the judgment, meanings or additional stories, instead allowing ourselves to simply experience them as neutral information that flows through us with ease.

Your personalized spiral stopper will help you to put on your observer hat, allowing you to step into your full potential as a conscious creator of your reality.

In order to shift into conscious creator mode, you must get through the initial 30-90 seconds of your fight or flight survival reaction without getting sucked into the spiral.

Note:

Stopping the spiral is NOT about distracting yourself or dissociating so that you can avoid facing your experiences and/or emotions. In order to properly process and release your emotions in a healthy way, you need to feel them and allow them to move through you.

Let's Build your Personalized Spiral Stopper

Everyone is unique and has different likes and dislikes. The key here is to build your spiral stopper toolbox with the tools that resonate *with you.* I encourage you to try out many of the tools to see which tools work well for you and which do not. This way, you can build a collection of tools that gives you enough variety to choose from when you're experiencing the start of a spiral.

By actively stopping the spiral with one or more of these techniques, you give your brain time to catch up to what is happening, become emotionally regulated and shift into a state where you will be able to intentionally create your experience rather than simply accepting the asshole mind's primitive reaction.

The following is a list of spiral stoppers that you can trial or add to your toolbox, but feel free to get creative and think outside the box, too!

Add your creative, outside-of-the-box ideas here:

My 'go-to' Spiral Stoppers

- Breathwork (as simple as counting your breath, or breathing in and out of your heart) and/or meditation (any style, including prayer) * see appendix to download your free spiral stopper breathwork and meditation practice
- Practice gratitude (really feeling into this to experience the emotion of gratitude)
- Spend a moment completing a full-body scan, becoming aware of the sensations in your body
- Go outside for sunshine and fresh air
- Grounding practices such as sound therapy or literally feet to earth (aka earthing)
- Spending time in nature

Quickies

- Smile the biggest smile you've ever smiled
- High-five yourself in the mirror (thanks Mel Robbins for this one!)
- Give yourself a hug
- Have a belly laugh
- Look at a photo/video that makes you feel good
- Play or sing a song that makes you feel good
- Choose a keyword or phrase such as "STOP!" or "STFU, Mind!"
- Cuddle or play with your pet
- Affirmations (that you fully believe are true) or a mantra
- Apply essential oils

- Ho'oponopono (a traditional Hawaiian practice of reconciliation and forgiveness)
- Have a healthy snack
- Read a book
- Brain dump/ write your to-do list
- Drink a glass of water or a cup of tea

Movement/touch-based spiral stoppers

- Seek out a hug from a loved one
- Shake your whole body
- Have a mini dance party
- Go for a walk, run or bike ride
- Yoga or other stretching
- Do some jumping jacks

- EFT tapping

- Self-massage or other self-touch (wink, wink)

- Havening

- Vagus nerve stimulation

More stoppers

- Have a shower or bath

- Go for a drive

- Journalling

- Talk with a trusted friend, coach, mentor or therapist

- Have a cold shower or splash cold water on your face

Getting the F*ck Unstuck

Implementing your Spiral Stopper

I suggest that you create a list of at least 5-6 spiral stopping tools and keep multiple copies of your list available while you're practicing and implementing. You will want to keep a copy handy in your phone, on your bathroom mirror, in your car, at your computer, in your kitchen and anywhere else that you are likely to experience a spiral. Be sure to include a variety of stoppers so that you're covered in many potential circumstances (such as when you're in public or somewhere with limited resources).

Remember, when faced with a spiral-inducing thought or emotion, you need to spend at least 30-90 seconds using one or more stoppers. As you recognize these challenging thoughts or emotions arising, refer to your list of spiral stoppers and choose one or more of the tools to implement immediately. In doing so, you can move your mind and body *through* the survival response and into conscious thinking.

As you start to practise using the tools, take note of those which work best for you so that you can quickly and easily apply them in the future. You may wish to update your list as you try any new tools, however, I've found that once you figure out what is working best for you consistently, you will probably be able to implement the tools and strategies without requiring the list.

I also want to point out that as you begin to work with this tool, you will most certainly be given the opportunity to practice. This means you will find challenging thoughts and emotions coming up, in order for you to put your new skills to use, and to get intentional. Sometimes, even those which you thought you had already dealt with, will also reappear. When old patterns resurface, this is a wonderful gift! In these moments, remember that although you're witnessing a familiar pattern, YOU are no longer the same and can now see everything from a much higher vantage point! Simply observe what is coming up and release what no longer serves your highest good. You are evolving!

With consistent and intentional application, you will find yourself far more frequently operating from the observer mode and having far fewer thought spirals. Your experience will continue to elevate as you embrace acceptance of what is. From this space, you can begin to get more creative with what you wish to experience and get down to making it all happen with much more ease and flow!

Becoming a Conscious Creator

Once you have gotten a consistent handle on the thought spirals, you can elevate this practice to more consistently act as the conscious creator that you already are.

It is crucial that you not simply avoid looking at that which is uncomfortable and overwhelming, and instead take the time to get curious about what keeps coming up. The way to move lovingly through uncomfortable thinking and emotions is by being mindful and getting truly curious.

Curiosity is Key

Outside of survival mode, you will have a much greater ability to be mindful - increasing awareness of your thoughts and emotions *before they trigger a survival mode response.*

With a calm and less judgmental approach and the lens of the observer, you can much more objectively assess what is coming up in its earliest stages. You may want to explore further into the origin of your spirals so that you can *actively get to work on moving through and releasing them.*

Here is an example of a journaling practice you may wish to explore. Note that it is typically best to address just one area at a time in greater depth and fully work through and clear it before starting to work on another.

Journaling prompts

- What is ONE triggering thought, idea, or experience to explore today?

- What emotion does it evoke in me?

- Where do I feel this in my body?

- When is the first time I remember having this experience or emotion?

- What did I most need at that moment?

- How can I give myself what I need at this moment?

- What might I need to forgive others for? (Note: more on forgiveness in an upcoming section)

- What emotions have I been carrying that aren't mine? (Can I now set them down/ release them?)

- What might I need to forgive myself for?

Support & Accountability

You may wish to enlist some support to help you with the implementation of this new tool, and to work through the processing of your thought patterns and emotions. This may be a spouse, trusted friend, mentor, therapist or coach with whom you feel completely safe to be yourself and with whom you will be heard and validated without judgment.

Even coaches and therapists have coaches and therapists because sometimes it is truly helpful to have someone with an outside, unbiased and fresh perspective. After all, when we are trying to create new habits, our brain is likely to revert to those old patterns and filter out things that don't align (sometimes including your new habits!). Sometimes an outside view can help you to see the limitless possibilities and opportunities that currently reside just outside the scope of your perception and to help keep you on track while you practice the art of being a conscious creator.

Reframing Limiting Beliefs and Mindsets

We all have many beliefs and mindsets running subconsciously without much of a thought. Many of these have come from early childhood before we were even consciously aware that we were taking in these beliefs. This includes your understanding of how the world works, what is "right and wrong", what is "good and bad", and your beliefs about other people and yourself.

Remember, your asshole mind does not operate in the space of looking at what is *good* or *best* for us, it acts only to keep us safe. It does its job by keeping our experience in line with those beliefs and mindsets because to our mind what is *familiar* is safe, and what is *uncertain* is unsafe. And as you know, when you desire to grow, that requires us to step outside of the familiar and face uncertainty. This requires intentional work to look at the actual function of our beliefs and mindsets.

Most often, when you are unable to effect lasting change in your life, it's because on some level you are benefiting from the status quo. Sometimes these "benefits" can be pretty sneaky, and often are not actually benefits at all.

For example, consider my client who I will call Lisa. Lisa has been overweight since childhood and, despite her best efforts, has continued to struggle with both her weight and her overall health. Lisa *knows* that it would be best for her to lose weight and that it would help her to eliminate some of her health concerns and bring others under control. She knows that losing weight would improve her life and her health significantly, yet she finds herself self-sabotaging and repeating less favorable health habits daily without fail. Sigh. Lisa then spirals out thinking that the whole thing is hopeless and then finds herself elbow-deep in a bag of potato chips and feeling both sick *and* guilty. Why can't she just stop herself and make the changes that she knows damn well would be best for her?

In our work together we discovered that somewhere in the background, Lisa has been running the script that excess weight is a protective barrier that will keep away the unwanted male attention that she experienced as a girl. Because as a girl these unwanted male gazes made her uncomfortable (brushed off by her parents and teachers who all told her it's no big deal, that's just how boys/men are), she turned to food for emotional comfort. 'If I'm overweight and unattractive, it'll stop', she had told herself. Her mind saw the excess weight as having the *perceived* benefit of making herself appear less attractive and thus less appealing to the male gaze. What began as a safety mechanism many years ago has been running on autopilot ever since.

Over the years, she's even taken to beating herself up via a constant dialogue of negative self-talk because she thought if she was just more dedicated and committed, she could finally get healthy. And there she was, attempting unsuccessfully to *guilt and trash talk* herself into making changes, while her health remained significantly affected. She felt like a complete and total failure.

But it's no wonder that she'd been unable to make a change when we look at those subconscious beliefs running below the surface on autopilot. She didn't truly believe that it was *safe* to lose weight. In fact, her desire to lose weight was completely incongruent with her core need to feel safe.

Upon taking a closer look, she realized that her size is actually *not* a deterrent for the male gaze, and it is still attracting attention, wanted or not. The line of reasoning that her asshole mind was using to keep her "safe" wasn't even keeping her safe, it was only keeping her in the familiar!

She also discovered that the guilt and trash talk were not actually motivating her to make changes as she'd expected. Instead of feeling fired up to move more and eat better, the guilt and shame she felt made her feel even *less* motivated to make changes. Around and around the patterns she went.

However, by using the tools to stop the spiral and become a conscious creator who objectively looked at these beliefs, Lisa was able to slowly break free of the patterns and make health choices that were better for her. As she implemented the tools that worked best for her, she learned how to make choices that made her *feel good.* The better she felt, the better her choices were. It was as though she had become a whole new person, someone who *felt good* and *was successfully making changes to become the highest version of herself.* She flipped the spiral into a positive one!

Lisa now has far more energy to play with her kids, is more productive at work, and more consistently makes health choices that support the experiences she desires to create. By stopping the spiral, she has significantly improved her relationship with food and exercise, as well as her relationship with herself and others.

I want to point out that these changes didn't simply happen overnight and Lisa didn't do this work alone, but I did want to share just how sneaky some of those underlying beliefs that keep us so fucking stuck in our patterns and habits can be - and how our need for (at least *perceived*) safety can trump all rational action if we aren't intentional about doing the work.

Once you've unpacked any underlying limiting beliefs and mindsets it is crucial to spend time reframing them. Flip the script and remind yourself often of what you *desire* to believe.

Believe it or Not

For you to experience something that you haven't before, it is crucial to hold the belief that you *can* have that experience.

What you don't believe possible will be very unlikely to come to fruition for two reasons:

1. You are unlikely to take action because you won't believe it's worthwhile
2. Your subconscious may work against you (aka self-sabotage) because your self-doubt makes it appear as though you do not truly want it

Sometimes the first step to belief is simply believing it is *possible,* even if you do not truly feel it is *likely.* Holding onto even a small likelihood can sometimes be enough to start taking the first small steps and leaning into the exciting zone of uncertainty where the limitless possibility exists.

Henry Ford said it best: "Whether you think you can, or think you can't, you are right."

You'll never have those experiences that you dream of if you don't even try!

Leaning into Uncertainty

As you face the unfamiliar yet expansive field of possibility that lies outside of what is currently known and certain, you are very likely to experience some discomfort. As you become practiced at stopping the spiral, you will be able to view this discomfort with an increasingly objective lens, thus even reducing your own experience of "discomfort".

As the observer, you can now take a more detached look at what this emotion being experienced is telling you and what to do about it. It allows you the ability to now assess whether taking a certain action feels *expansive* to you or whether it feels *restrictive*. Because both fear and excitement produce a similar physiological reaction within your body (increased breathing and heart rate), it is important to do this assessment because as a conscious creator *you can now choose how you would like to label this feeling based on what you know to be true for you, rather than simply allowing your mind to label it as "fear" in another asshole attempt to keep you "safe".* When you *know* (aka you trust your intuition) that something is for your best and highest good and that taking steps to create that experience feels expansive to you, you can now label this emotion as excitement and step boldly into the unknown of uncertainty and a whole new world of possibility! And trust me, life can become absolutely fucking magical!

Become a Solution-Seeker

When you focus on your problems, you actually end up keeping yourself stuck in suffering. By allowing your energy to flow towards your challenges, you have far less energy available to come up with creative solutions. By taking your focus off of blaming, complaining and excuses, you can shift yourself into creative solution-seeking mode.

As you implement and practice using your personalized spiral stopper, you will become more skilled at shutting down any solution-avoidant behaviors that have been running on autopilot, freeing up mental space for discovering creative solutions. By using it regularly you will become able to more objectively see your role, take responsibility for your contribution, and operate in an increasingly conscious manner. Instead of focusing on what has happened in the past, you will be far better able to stay present in the current moment where you are creating your current experience. This is where your most creative ideas will flow from, unhindered by the constriction of the certain, now open to the limitless possibilities that exist.

What you Resist Persists

By attempting to resist feeling certain emotions or what we deem to be uncomfortable experiences, we actually must place our attention on them. Where our attention flows, our energy goes and the more we attempt to avoid things, the more attention we give them and thus the more permission we are giving them to remain in our lives. In doing so, we in fact hold onto those emotions and experiences that we do not want, rather than moving through them.

Want to let go for good so that you can stop experiencing more of what you *don't want*?

Get curious about your emotions, thoughts, and patterns and then if necessary take appropriate action.

When experiencing uncomfortable emotions or situations, remember that you always have the choice to:

1. Avoid it (a terrible idea for the reasons above)
2. Accept it as is
3. Release it (either let it go or reframe it) or
4. Take action to change it

Similar to shifting out of problem-seeking mode and into solution-seeking mode, setting your energy and emotions on what you *do want* is in fact the fastest way to attain it.

Triggers are Merely Information

From time to time you are likely to experience "automatic" nervous system responses to something or someone else. When this happens, it may catch you off guard, or induce a spiral. As a conscious creator, I want you to know that *this is completely normal!* But, going forward you are going to flip the script on being triggered and instead put on your detached observer hat: triggers are merely information being brought to your attention.

Until you attach meaning, stories, beliefs, and emotion to them... these triggers are merely things coming up for you to take a closer look at.

The best way to deal with triggers is to stop the spiral and consciously look at your response with a childlike curiosity. In time, this process will become increasingly easy as you practice leaving judgement aside.

Self Care isn't Selfish

It is not selfish to care for yourself well, in fact you are best able to care for and love others when you have built a foundation of unconditional self love and acceptance. By taking good care of yourself you become stronger, healthier, and happier and as a result, you increase your capacity to give to and care for others.

While it's important not to be overly dependent on another (your experience is YOUR responsibility), we aren't meant to do life alone. Community and connection is crucial, yet in today's society we can often feel like a burden if we seek support from another. However, by learning to ask for what you need and giving yourself permission to receive, you not only create opportunities for others to serve you (a gift to them!) but your needs are better taken care of (win-win!).

If you want to experience your best for the long term, you absolutely MUST take good care of yourself and put yourself first at times. As you give yourself the radical self love and acceptance that you crave, you begin to build an abundance of love and acceptance from which you are able to give. Having this solid foundation will impact all relationships in your life!

The Healing Power of Forgiveness

You have within you a magical ability to rewire your brain (create new neural pathways with your thoughts) and improve your overall health and happiness (changing your body's physiological response). One piece of this involves releasing thoughts or emotions that are limiting you, and one practice in particular has the potential to completely change your life: radical forgiveness.

The practice of forgiveness is designed to help cultivate compassion for both yourself and for others, increase your empathy, and help you to release negative energies that are keeping you stuck.

Forgiveness is not about letting the other person off the hook or forgetting about what happened. Letting go of stuck emotions that no longer serve you is for *your* benefit and therefore this practice does not require any apology or even acknowledgement from the other party.

It can be beneficial to remember that everyone is operating at their best given the resources and experiences they have and have had. Remember the old adage "hurting people hurt people"? When you remember that those who have hurt you have also been hurt, it can help you to look at them and the situation with greater compassion and this can in fact help to diminish your discomfort whether it be from fear, anger, frustration or other painful emotions. When you look at your own guilt and shame, it is also important to remember that *you were also just doing the best you could with the resources you had.* You deserve compassion, too.

Consider a time when you yourself have lashed out in pain and either intentionally or unintentionally hurt another. What you truly needed in that moment of pain was LOVE. ACCEPTANCE. SAFETY. These are some of your most basic human needs, and when these are not met, it is easy to end up operating out of fear, attempting to protect ourselves.

What we truly need when we have made a mistake is not a lecture or an angry response, but rather compassion, understanding, and support so that we can learn from our mistakes and do things differently next time. What we need is more love, not less.

Unfortunately, we don't always receive this type of compassionate and loving response or support from those around us and if we are not careful, these fear-based behaviours may become all too common as we strive to create safety for ourselves.

The good news is that you can create for yourself this very love and safety that you require and desire. It doesn't need to come from anything that is outside of ourselves, in fact it already exists in abundance within us. And what you give to the world, the world gives back to you.

Punishing yourself repeatedly for your mistakes is a waste of time and energy, and you deserve to live a life free and clear of ongoing guilt or shame. You've suffered plenty long enough. It's time to swap this suffering for self-love and acceptance!

To be clear, this does NOT mean that you must forget what others have done or allow them to further mistreat you. It also doesn't mean that you can simply forgive and move on instantly. Forgiveness is a process that can sometimes take time. It is worth noting again that, depending on your circumstances, forgiveness in the traditional sense will likely feel like an impossible task. However, radical forgiveness has nothing to do with them and everything to do with healing yourself.

It is crucial to create and uphold strong personal boundaries *in order to teach others how to treat you with love.* Good boundaries will serve to protect you from further mistreatment and unnecessary suffering.

Increasing our empathy means that we can begin to see things from another's perspective, even if it differs from our own. You will find that this empathy expands even more quickly when you have built a solid foundation of self-love and acceptance based on having and practicing empathy with and for yourself.

A Journey to Self-love and Acceptance

The fastest way to experience your highest and best life is sometimes the hardest for people to get on board with because it requires radical self-love and acceptance they may not be familiar with.

This means accepting things as they are while continuing to work towards your ideal experience. You do not need to be content with the way things are to simply accept that this is in fact where you are *right now*. Giving yourself love and compassion will fuel your growth journey so much faster than continuing to beat yourself up, I promise!

You and you alone are responsible for creating the experiences that you have in your life. And while you may not be able to control the external circumstances around you, you *always* get to choose who you will be in response.

The more you love and accept yourself as a whole human, flaws and all, the better you will be at extending that very same unconditional love and compassion to others. And when you can begin to do this, you will soon be able to surrender to what is, and simply ride the waves of life while creating your own experience.

Creating happiness is possible at all times... even in the mundane moments of the daily routine. As you continue to practice your skills as a conscious creator you will even begin finding joy and happiness in your struggles as you begin to see challenges as *opportunities for growth,* and failures as *feedback.*

Next Steps

Now that you've begun your growth journey by learning how to stop yourself from spiraling, you can use this momentum to consciously create more and more of absolutely everything you desire.

Gaining Momentum

As someone who has a busy mind that loves to have a detailed plan of *alllllll of the how* nailed down before taking action, this is something that has revolutionized my ability to move past the overwhelm and into intentional action. The reality is, that you actually *can't* know the entire path from the start. The harder you try to make things feel certain, the more you will experience challenges and reminders that the *best possibilities and opportunities* lie outside of what is certain.

The secret to creating more of what you want involves setting your target destination, determining *just the very first smallest step,* and then *surrendering to the uncertainty.* You will find that if you agonize over the details of the *how* before you begin, you will often remain stuck. If this is something that you struggle with, it can be really helpful to have some support to help you stay focused on the next step.

The more attached to outcomes you are, the more stuck you will feel, and the greater the disappointment you will experience if things do not go according to plan. The more detached from outcomes that you are, the more creative you will be and the greater the variety of new possibilities that you *hadn't even thought of* will appear right before your very eyes.

Note:

You will also be more aware of the things which no longer align. They may well stand out like a sore thumb now that you have begun the work. Do not for a moment feel like your progress is lost when you see the patterns arise. They are simply arising for you to work through and to verify your new experience as someone who is intentional! Observe them for the opportunity they are to see things in a new light and thank them for reminding you who you truly are before letting them go.

When making goals and setting intentions (a goal is more outcome based whereas an intention is more experiential), you may want to consider what is within your control and what lies outside of your control, and structure your intentions in such a way that you alone can create the experience for yourself without reliance on external sources. You will find that when you create goals that rely heavily on someone else's input, you will often find yourself waiting around for someone else to make your goals happen. This is not very empowering. However, when you set intentions instead, you place the onus on YOURSELF. This empowers you to get out there and make it happen. The steps don't need to be huge, they just need to be consistent enough to make forward momentum.

Don't forget, practice makes progress!

Celebrate your Success!

Celebrating small wins along the way (no matter how insignificant they may seem) can help you to keep your positive momentum as you work towards your goals and intentions. For example, learning how to make your own coffee when an ex-partner always made it for you can seem small but can feel extremely empowering. Each time that you make your coffee can be a reminder of the progress you've made towards becoming independent and self-sufficient!

The more you celebrate how far you've come, the more motivation and momentum you will continue to create for yourself. Besides, constantly looking at your goals and then beating yourself up for not being there yet sure wasn't working, was it?

The more you focus on what's going well and how much progress you're making, the less often you're going to find your 'asshole mind' running the show. You might even discover that your mind can become an ally helping to cheer you on towards making *all* of your dreams come true, creating an upward spiral of happiness!

What's one thing you can celebrate today that will help you to reflect on the progress you've made so far? Take a moment right now and celebrate!

Final Thoughts

In case you needed a reminder today:

You are soooo loved (flaws and all)

You are soooo worthy (simply for being YOU)

And you have alllll of the power to make it happen for yourself!

Now get out there and start creating your very best life!

♡ Christy

Appendix: More Inspiration and Information

An Important Note about your Mental Health

If you have suffered a significant trauma or have diagnosed mental health issues that are impacting your day-to-day life, or if you are ever at risk of harming yourself or others, please reach out to a qualified professional (therapist, counselor, psychologist, doctor, etc.) If you are in immediate danger, please call 9-1-1. For mental health support:

In Canada: Call 1-866-585-0445 or text WELLNESS to:

- 686868 for youth / 741741 for adults

In the U.S.A.: Suicide & Crisis Lifeline - Call or text #988

Crisis Text Line - Text "HELLO" to 741741

Disaster Distress Helpline - Call or text 1-800-985-5990

Freebies

Visit www.gtfu.ca to grab the following freebies:

- printable PDF version of the Spiral Stopper Template
- spiral stopper meditation
- Conscious Creator Guided Meditation
- Guided Visualization of Future Self

Feedback

I would love to hear from you- if you have 3-5 minutes to provide some feedback about this project, please send me an email at hello@coachchristyholt.com.

Create Your Happy Podcast

For more inspiration and a deeper dive into many of these topics and more, please check out my podcast, *Create Your Happy*, which is available wherever you listen to podcasts (links available at www.createyourhappy.ca)

Facebook Communities

Get The F*ck Unstuck with Coach Christy - for conscious creators who want to be more intentional about creating the experiences they desire.

The Conscious Creators Collective - for change makers and impact leaders looking to connect, collaborate, create and celebrate in life, business and relationship.

Coaching & Support

If you could benefit from the additional support and would like to learn more about how you can deepen your journey as a conscious creator, you can find the details about my current coaching programs at www.coachchristyholt.com/coaching.

All of my programs are built around my signature CREATE Method:

C.alibrate your Consciousness: get curious about your beliefs and identity, and recalibrate them so that you can begin to create from the unlimited power of your conscious self.

R.efine your Routine: tweak your routine in order to create the most conducive environment for your success to be created.

E.levate your Energy: boost your energy through intentional work around healing and increasing your frequency to harmonize your mind-body-soul connection and operate from the energy of unconditional love.

A.ctivate your Aligned Life: connect with your unique space of beingness in order to rediscover and then confidently embody who you truly are and what your purpose is.

T.une in to your true Vision: discover how to align your actions to your higher self identity, and unlock new possibilities as you step into what feels most expansive to your soul.

E.mpower your elevated self: truly embody your next level self, operate from a higher level of consciousness and become unf*ckwithable so that nothing can stop your ability to create impact in the world.

Affirmations for Beginners – Mini Cheat Sheet

When it comes to affirmations, stating things that you don't truly believe is a waste of time. Affirmations will only be effective when you can say them with emotion and belief, and sometimes that can be near impossible when there are obvious reminders in your day-to-day life to show you just how far away you are from the truth as you state your affirmations. So, if you aren't yet feeling able to stand behind the affirmations that your future self would make, here are a couple of hacks.

Instead of saying "I am ___", you can use one of these modifiers to make your affirmations feel more congruent with where you are currently at:

I am learning how to___

I am going to become___

I am in the process of _____

I desire to _____

I am creating (the experience of) _____

Just for today I _____

Or even the UBER truthful version:

I don't know how to _____ and *that's okay because I can and will learn.*

THE SPIRAL STOPPER

Complete this template for as many scenarios as necessary and place copies around the spaces where you most commonly experience these spirals and overwhelm. You may also want to take a photo and keep it on your phone for quick reference on the go!

When I start to feel or think _____

I am going to immediately execute one or more of the following spiral stoppers (60-90 seconds+):

1. _____

2. _____

3. _____

4. _____

5. _____

Once I have executed one or more spiral stopper, the thought reframe I wish to implement is: _____

_____

Additional notes: _____

_____

_____

download a printable PDF copy at www.gtfu.ca

About the Author

Christy Holt is a self proclaimed
happiness hussy, adventure guide,
mentor/ coach, podcast host (Create Your Happy), and author
who is passionate about empowering others to CREATE the
happy life, relationship and impact that their soul desires.

We are all powerful creators of our own experience and
through the use of her signature CREATE method, Christy loves
to guide people as they learn how to create for themselves the
happiness that they are so deserving of!

Connect: www.coachchristyholt.com

Book website: www.gtfu.ca

www.gtfu.ca